Lindsay Barrett George

AROUND THE WORLD

Who's Been Here?

GREENWILLOW BOOKS NEW YORK

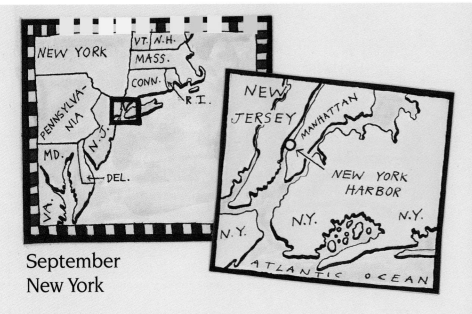

September
New York

Hello, Class,

At last! Here I am on the first leg of my trip, thanks to my Circumnavigation-of-the-Globe Grant. I have my camera and sketch pad in hand, and I hope to see many of the animals that we talked about and studied in our science classes.

I promise to report to you throughout our nine-month expedition. I will miss you all, but I look forward to seeing lots of new places and making lots of new friends.

With anticipation,
Miss Lewis

A final wave good-bye

Our ship, Explorer—home for the next nine months

October
Peru

I found this tapir in the stream near our hut.

Dear Class,

Our ship, *Explorer*, left New York harbor and sailed south to the Panama Canal. A Canal Zone pilot navigated the ship through the locks. It took us about eight hours to reach the Pacific Ocean. Then we headed for the South American city of Lima on the coast of Peru.

We boarded a small plane and flew to Puerto Maldonado, a town on the Madre de Dios River. Motorized canoes took us to the Tambopata Research Center. As we approached the Center, we heard loud howling. We were told it came from the howler monkeys that live in the neighboring rain forest.

Early the next morning we traveled to the grayish-pink clay cliffs that rise over the bank of the river. I put my hand against the rough surface of a cliff and felt the large, scoop-shaped gouges that covered it.

Who's been here?

Adiós, amigas y amigos,
Señorita Lewis

Our hut in the reserve

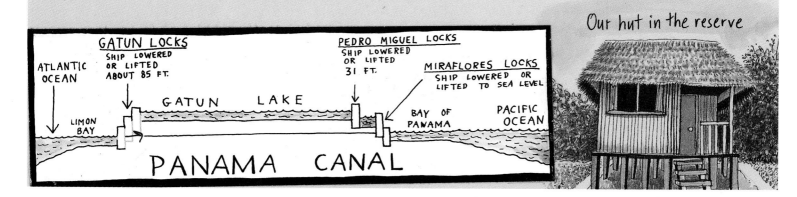

A noisy howler monkey

The grayish-pink cliffs on the river

A hungry river otter

These are the gouges in the cliffs.

Macaws.

An orca breaches behind our ship.

November
Elephant Island

Hello, Class,

Our ship traveled down the west coast of South America and headed for the northern extension of the Antarctic Peninsula. Seals and Antarctic terns followed us. I saw orca and minke whales searching for food in the cold waters.
Helicopters took us to Elephant Island. Along the rocky coast we found hundreds of saucer-shaped mounds of pebbles.

Who's been here?

Until next time,
Miss Lewis

The pack ice in front of _Explorer_

An elephant seal pops up for air.

A tern

The mounds
of pebbles

Adélie penguins.

Waving from our hot-air balloon!

December
Amboseli National Park

Hi, Class,

Explorer left the chilly waters of Antarctica and sailed northeast for warmer climes. Kenya in East Africa was our next stop. Safari vehicles took us west into Amboseli National Park. We could see the snowcap of Mt. Kilimanjaro in Tanzania as we approached the park.

We woke up at dawn to watch the animals feeding before it became too hot. A group of zebras grazed near a swamp. Then they cautiously approached the water's edge.

We were able to view parts of the preserve from a hot-air balloon. We waved at Masai herdsmen who were leading their cattle to a river, and they waved back. I saw trees from which the bark had been stripped.

Who's been here?

Kwaheri,
Miss Lewis

A Masai herdsman and me

A vervet monkey and her infant

Some thirsty, early-morning swamp visitors

An ostrich tries to lead us away from her nest.

A tree stripped bare

The ostrich nest

An African
elephant
and
her calf.

Our camp on a snow-covered mountain slope

January
China

Dear Class,

We traveled by plane from Africa to China, to the Wolong Natural Reserve near the Pitiao River.

We left camp early in the morning, after a breakfast of rice gruel with roasted peanuts and pickled vegetables, hot tea, and a type of thin bread called mantou. We hiked up a path into the mountains. A Himalayan cuckoo called out its morning greeting, "Boo-boo-boo." Our Chinese guide pointed to a pile of husks in a small clearing between stalks of bamboo. Farther up the trail Jay Weiss, one of the teachers in our group, discovered two pale green objects that lay at the base of a hollow in a fir tree. They were oblong in shape, about six inches by two inches in size.

"Daxiongmao!" our guide said excitedly.

Who's been here?

Zaigian pengyou,
Miss Lewis

The husks of bamboo shoots in a pile

I drew this gentle-looking takin bull while he was browsing some plants around our camp.

I saw this lesser panda eating in a tree.

Jay Weiss holding two pale green objects at the base of a hollow fir tree

A giant panda and her cub.

A curious squirrel

February
Japan

Hello, Class,

It is hard to believe, but my around-the-world trip is half over. We met *Explorer* in the Chinese city of Shanghai and headed northeast to the island of Honshu, in Japan.
Our ship docked near Tokyo, and we backpacked into the snow-topped mountains north of the city. During an early morning hike I heard chattering squirrels playing tag in the trees. Many of the evergreens were bare of their needles.
I found a packed-down path leading from tree to tree. I was surprised to see snowballs scattered around the edges of some hot springs. There were no human footprints in the snow.

Who's been here?

Sayonara,
Miss Lewis

Our ship,
Explorer,
in the shadow
of Mt. Fuji

I found this packed-down path in the snow.

I wondered why some trees had no bark.

The mysterious snowballs!

Japanese macaques.

A wombat

March
Australia

Hi, everybody,

Our ship reached the eastern shore of Australia after some rough days at sea. Land Rovers took us to a wildlife sanctuary near Canberra. Emus ran alongside our cars, and white cockatoos cried, "B*rrrrarrrk.*" Wombats waddled away, ignoring our vehicles. When we looked up into the eucalyptus trees, we saw koalas slowly munching on the small, round leaves.

As I gazed at the golden, grassy plains in front of me, I heard a grunt and a thump from under a tree.

Who's been here?

Hope you are all having a bonzer time,
Miss Lewis

Peggy Trimpi,
a fellow teacher,
cuddles a young
wombat.

This crimson rosella
greeted us
with its morning song.

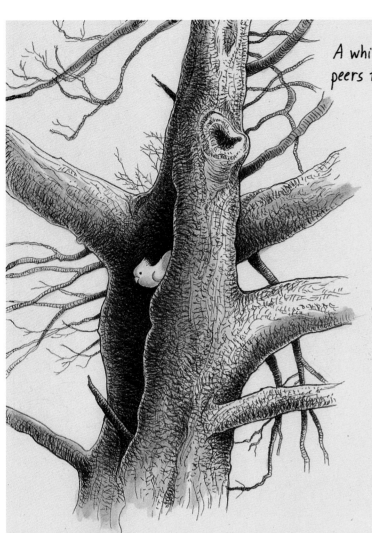

A white cockatoo
peers from its nest.

An emu

Trying to get a closer look at a koala and her cub

A gray kangaroo
and her joey.

These Dall sheep kept us company.

April
Alaska

Dear Class,

Explorer navigated north for several weeks and passed through the unpredictable and stormy waters surrounding the Aleutian Islands. Our boat docked south of Anchorage in Alaska. We drove to the Visitor Access Center in Denali National Park. Shuttle buses carried us into the heart of the park.

John Ross, a bush pilot, flew three of us over the Cathedral Spires to a ranger station. A ranger, Karen Boyle, joined us on our trip back. White Dall sheep watched us from rocky ledges. As we hiked over steep mountain passes, we found trails cut into the tundra.

"Sheep?" I asked.

Karen shook her head.

"No," she said. "Listen."

I faintly heard the sound of clicking. As we climbed higher, the clicking grew louder and louder. Soon I heard thousands of clicks.

Who's been here?

See you soon,
Miss Lewis

I saw this grizzly and her cub from the shuttle bus.

The view was spectacular as we flew in front of Mt. McKinley.

I photographed Karen tagging a golden eaglet. (It's not as big as it looks!)

The trail cut into the rocky tundra

A herd of barren-ground caribou.

May
California

This gull landed on the railing of our ship.

My dear friends,

As I approach the end of my trip, I know that the people I met and the animals I saw will stay with me forever. Each animal species, each one of us, is very special. Today it is more important than ever to show kindness to all animals, and to each other.

As our ship headed down the coast of California, we sighted Año Nuevo Island. Looking through my binoculars, I saw hundreds of tan rocks on the island. The rocks turned out to be Steller sea lions, staking out territories on their favorite reefs. It was a thrilling sight!

A fellow shipmate called out, "Position, three o'clock!"

A group of us hurried over to find out what was happening.

A circle of frothy water was visible off the right side of the ship. It was a watery footprint.

Who's been here?

Fondly,
Miss Lewis

On our last day in Alaska, I paddled this kayak as we left the Kenai Fjords. The water was too icy to fall in.

The tan rocks that moved

The watery footprint

A humpback whale
and her calf.

Dear Students,
I found this caribou antler lying in a patch of bearberry leaves on the Alaskan tundra. Who's been here?

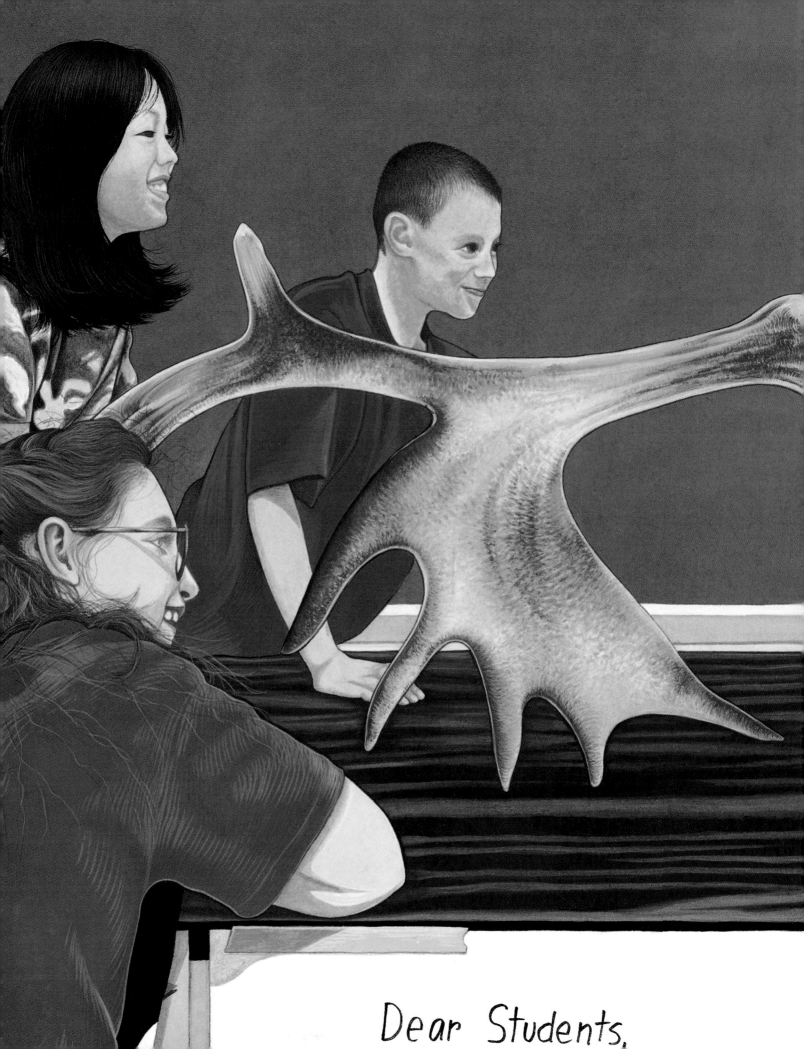

Dear Students,

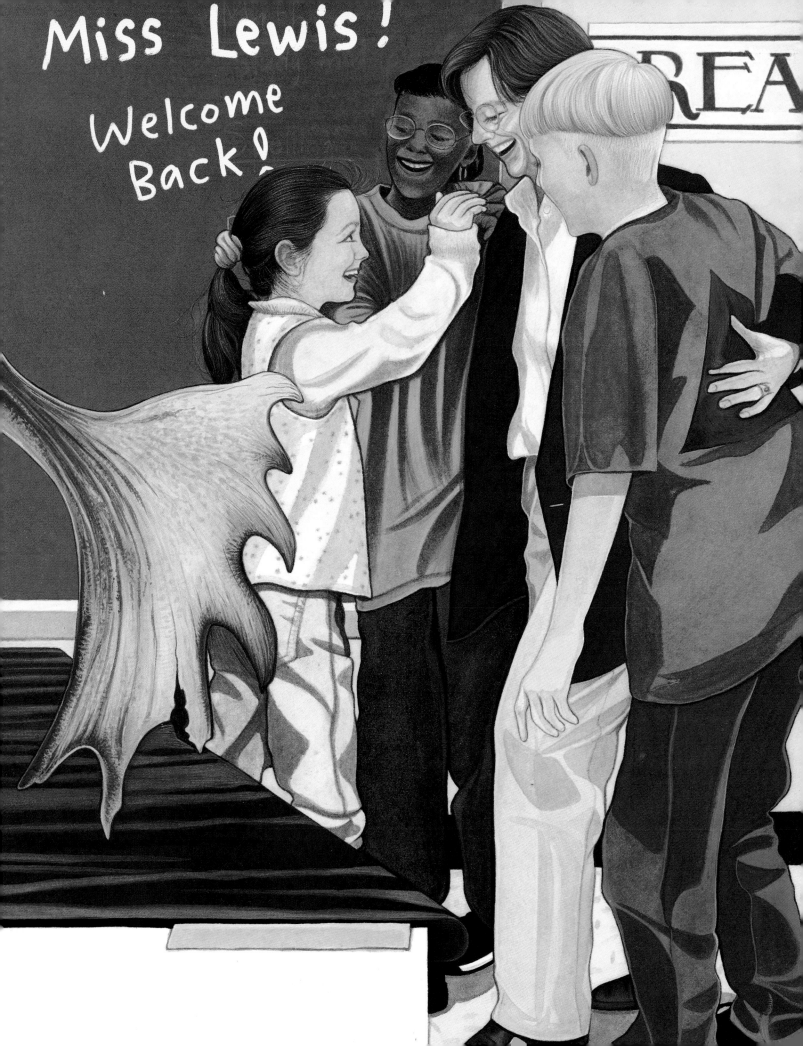

These brightly colored **macaws** are eating clay from a riverbank on the Tambopata River. Thousands of parrots from more than a dozen species visit this clay lick every day. Macaws eat the pulp of some fruits, and sometimes flowers and leaves, but seeds are their favorite food. The clay neutralizes toxic compounds found in the seeds and provides salts and minerals the birds need.

These **Japanese macaques** (muh-KAKS), sometimes called "snow monkeys," are gathered around a hot spring. Two of the macaques sit in the steaming water, grooming each other and enjoying a warm bath. The other two are holding snowballs, which they've made. Macaques nibble on, play with, and carry snowballs, but they have not been known to throw them.

An **Adélie penguin** sits on its nest of stones while its mate stands guard. In the Antarctic spring, the male Adélie arrives first at the rookery (a place where birds gather to nest) to collect stones for the nest. When the female arrives, the pair scratch out a hollow in the ground for their eggs and line it with stones. After the eggs are laid, the male and female share the duty of sitting on the nest.

A mother **gray kangaroo** flees from her nest of grass, carrying her baby (called a "joey") in her pouch. In the midday heat kangaroos take naps under trees or rest on their haunches in the shade. The only vocal sounds these animals make are coughs or grunts. But when they feel threatened, they thump an alarm with their hind legs to warn other kangaroos of danger.

This **African elephant** cow is stripping the bark from an acacia tree with her tusks. An elephant must eat hundreds of pounds of plants, grasses, leaves, fruits, seeds, bark, and roots each day in order to stay alive. The five-month-old calf will learn which plants to eat by following and eating alongside its mother.

This herd of **barren-ground caribou** is headed for its calving grounds high in the mountains of Denali National Park. Both male and female caribou have antlers, and their usual movement is trotting. When caribou trot, the movement of their tendons slipping over sesamoid bones or cartilage produces a clicking sound.

This **giant panda** is lying with her cub in their den inside a hollow fir tree. Bamboo is the main food of giant pandas, who strip the outer layers of bamboo shoots before eating the tender centers. The pale green objects in front of the tree are panda droppings, which consist mainly of undigested bamboo stems. The droppings smell sweet, like freshly cut grass.

This **humpback whale**, seen with her calf, has just made a deep dive. Humpback whales arch their backs more than any other whale when they dive. When this one arched her back to dive, the flat parts of her tail, called the flukes, lifted above the water's surface. The flukes, which are about ten to twelve feet wide, left a clear circle of rising water, a "footprint."

Gouache paints were used for the full-color art. The text type is Novarese Book. Copyright © 1999 by Lindsay Barrett George. All rights reserved. No part of this book may be reproduced or utilized in any form or by any means, electronic or mechanical, including photocopying, recording, or by any information storage and retrieval system, without permission in writing from the Publisher, Greenwillow Books, a division of William Morrow & Company, Inc., 1350 Avenue of the Americas, New York, NY 10019. Printed in Singapore by Tien Wah Press   First Edition   10   9   8   7   6   5   4   3

Library of Congress Cataloging-in-Publication Data
George, Lindsay Barrett. Around the world : who's been here? / by Lindsay Barrett George.   p.   cm.   Summary: A teacher travels around the world viewing animals in their natural habitats and writes back to her class about her findings.   ISBN 0-688-15268-6 (trade).   ISBN 0-688-15269-4 (lib. bdg.).   [1. Animals—Fiction.   2. Voyages around the world—Fiction.   3. Letters—Fiction.]   I. Title.   PZ7.G29334At 1999   [E]—dc21   97-11200   CIP   AC

For John Wilde,
who taught me how to draw

My special thanks to Judy Weiss for her invaluable travel expertise;
Joseph Kowalski, Superintendent of the Milton Area School District,
for generously making available his school's facilities and students;
Elizabeth Lewis, who endured countless photo sessions with good humor,
and Elizabeth Shub, a valued companion on this journey.

Thanks also to Brian Batten, Karen Boyle, Cindy Gabriel, Margaret T. George,
Fred Beers, Zachary Edinger, Courtney Landis, Michael Longenberger,
Jacob Musser, Laci Newsome, Beth Reuthner, Sara Taggert, Jay Weiss,
Kim Whitman, Cindy Wilcox, and finally my family, Cammy, William, and Bill,
without whom this trip could not have been possible.

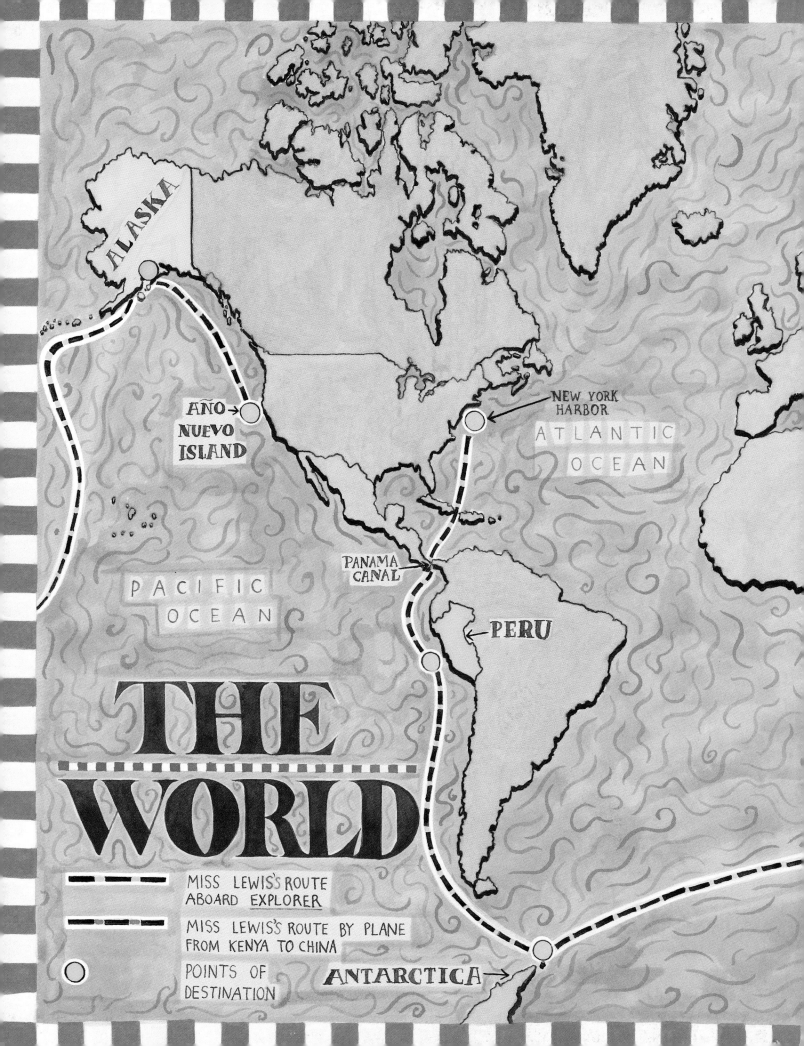

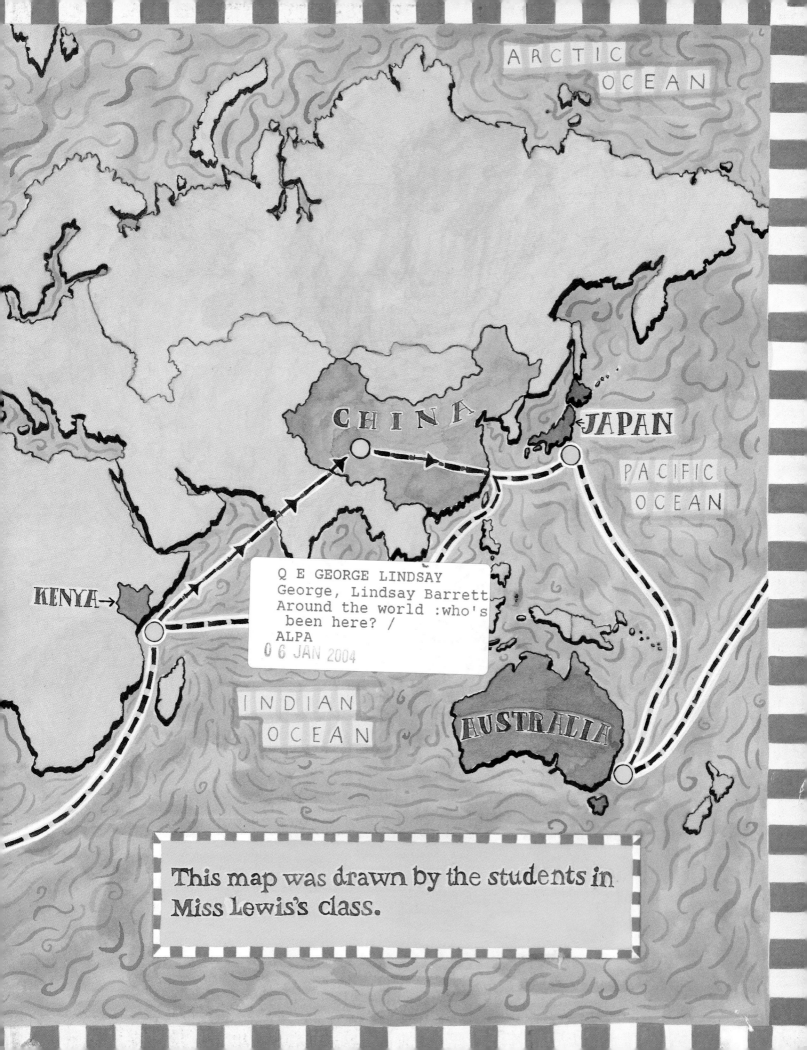

ARCTIC
OCEAN

CHINA

→JAPAN

PACIFIC
OCEAN

KENYA→

Q E GEORGE LINDSAY
George, Lindsay Barrett
Around the world :who's
    been here? /
ALPA
0 6 JAN 2004

INDIAN
OCEAN

AUSTRALIA

This map was drawn by the students in
Miss Lewis's class.